Science In Your Life:
MAGNETS
Sticking Together

Wendy Sadler

www.raintreepublishers.co.uk

Visit our website to find out more information about **Raintree** books.

To order:
☎ Phone 44 (0) 1865 888112
🖹 Send a fax to 44 (0) 1865 314091
🖥 Visit the Raintree bookshop at **www.raintreepublishers.co.uk** to browse our catalogue and order online.

First published in Great Britain by Raintree,
Halley Court, Jordan Hill, Oxford OX2 8EJ,
part of Harcourt Education.
Raintree is a registered trademark
of Harcourt Education Ltd.

Editorial: Melanie Copland, Kate Buckingham,
and Lucy Beevor
Design: Victoria Bevan
and Bridge Creative Services Ltd
Picture Research: Hannah Taylor
and Catherine Bevan
Production: Duncan Gilbert

Originated by Chroma Graphics (Overseas) Pte. Ltd
Printed and bound in China by
South China Printing Company

ISBN 1 844 43664 0
10 09 08 07 06
10 9 8 7 6 5 4 3 2 1

**British Library Cataloguing in
Publication Data**
Sadler, Wendy
Magnets. – (Science in your life)
538.4
A full catalogue record for this book is available
from the British Library.

Acknowledgements
Alamy Images pp. 26 (Brand X Pictures), 11 (Mitch
Diamond), 21 (Rex Argent), 22 (sciencephotos), 15
(Tetra Images), 25 (Thinkstock); Corbis pp. 27 (Mark
M. Lawrence); Corbis Royalty Free p. 16; Getty
Images p.17 (PhotoDisc); Harcourt Education Ltd
p.10, pp.4, 5, 6, 8, 9, 12, 13, 14, 18, 23, 29 (Tudor
Photography); Science Photo Library p.19 (Simon
Fraser).

Cover photograph of a horseshoe magnet
and metal filings reproduced with permission
of Getty/PhotoDisc.

Every effort has been made to contact copyright
holders of any material reproduced in this book.
Any omissions will be rectified in subsequent
printings if notice is given to the publishers.

The paper used to print this book comes from
sustainable resources.

Disclaimer
All the Internet addresses (URLs) given in this book
were valid at the time of going to press. However,
due to the dynamic nature of the Internet, some
addresses may have changed, or sites may have
changed or ceased to exist since publication. While
the author and publishers regret any inconvenience
this may cause readers, no responsibility for any
such changes can be accepted by either the author
or the publishers.

An adult should supervise all of the activities in
this book.

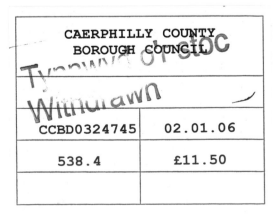

Contents

Any words appearing in the text in bold, **like this**, are explained in the glossary.

What are magnets?

Magnets are special **materials** that can stick to other magnets, or to some metals. Magnets are usually made of metal, but they can be made using other things, too.

Two magnets can either pull together or push apart. A magnet makes a **force** that can be felt by another magnet even if the magnets are not touching. We call this force **magnetism**.

These fridge magnets stick on the fridge door because it is metal.

magnets

There are magnets all around fridge or freezer doors. These help to keep the doors shut tight.

You might not realize it, but magnets and magnetism are all around you! Have you seen or used any of these today?

- You can stick messages to metal **surfaces**, such as fridges, using magnets.
- Magnets are used to make **electricity**.
- Cars and buses have electric **motors** that use magnetism.
- A computer has a magnetic disc inside called the hard disk.

What are magnets made of?

Magnetic **material** has a metal called **iron** inside it. Today, magnets are made using a mix of metals.

Some materials, such as plastic, glass, and **aluminium**, can never become magnetic. Magnets that look like they are made of plastic have tiny bits of iron in them to make them magnetic. If they were only made of plastic then they would not stick to metal, or to each other.

Magnets come in all shapes and sizes. Do you have any magnets like these in your house?

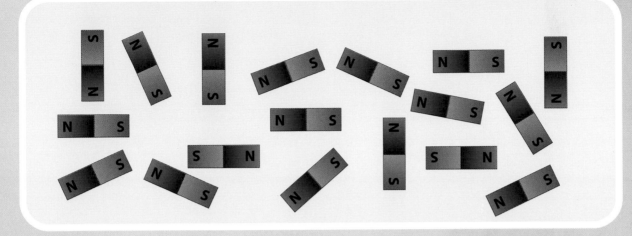

Materials that are magnetic are made up of many tiny magnets called **magnetic domains**. When these are pointing in lots of different directions, the material does not act like a magnet. This means it will not stick to another magnet.

When most of the magnetic domains are pointing in the same direction, the material does act like a magnet. It will stick to another magnet.

All magnets have two different ends. These ends are called the north and south poles. If you have two magnets and you bring them close together, the north pole of one will pull towards the south pole of the other.

Poles that are different are attracted to each other, so they pull together. This is called an **attractive force**.

North

South

Magnets come in different shapes but they all have a north and a south pole.

South

North

If you try to push the north pole of one magnet against the north pole of another magnet, they will not want to meet. We say that there is a **repulsive force** between them. This means that they try to push apart.

These magnets are floating in the air because there is a north pole pushing against a north pole, and then a south pole pushing against a south pole. The magnetic force keeps them apart.

Magnets in your life!

Find two magnets. Can you hold them in a way that they are attracted to (pull towards) each other? Can you hold them in a way that they are repelled (pushed away) from each other?

Sticky stuff

Magnets can stick to other magnets and to some types of metal. You can use a magnet to find out if objects are magnetic.

Magnets in your life!

Find a magnet and see which of the following things it will stick to:

- metal kitchen sink
- plastic
- hair
- heating pipe
- drink can
- taps
- wood.

All of these drink cans will be melted down and used again.

Magnets can be used to sort things. Some drink cans are made of a metal called **steel** and others are made from **aluminium**. When you **recycle** your cans they need to be sorted into the correct metal so they can be melted down and reused.

If a magnet sticks to a can then it is made of steel. If a magnet will not stick then it is made of aluminium. Some recycling factories use huge magnets to sort magnetic **material** from non-magnetic material.

Hold on!

When a magnet sticks to a piece of metal, the metal also becomes a magnet! We say that the metal has become **magnetized**. This means that you can then stick another piece of metal on to it and make a long magnetic chain.

Magnets in your life!

Stick a paper clip on to a magnet. The paper clip is now magnetized, and you will be able to stick another one to it. How long can you make the dangling chain of paper clips?

Magnets can sometimes be useful when you want to hold something in place. You can stick a drawing on a fridge door by putting the paper in between the magnet and the door. The **attractive force** between the magnet and the metal door is strong enough to hold the paper in place.

Can you see the magnets that are used to hold the train carriages together?

Magnetic Earth

Earth is like a giant magnet. There is hot **melted iron** inside Earth. This iron makes lines of **magnetism** around Earth. This is called Earth's **magnetic field**.

If you have a magnet that can swing and point in any direction it will line itself up with the magnetic field of Earth. This is how a **compass** works.

14

A magnet always points towards the north pole of Earth as long as no other magnets are close by. Other magnets can push or pull the magnet away from pointing north.

The magnetism in a compass means that you can always find out which way north is.

Magnetism and living things

Most people cannot feel the **magnetic field** of Earth, but some animals can! Some birds fly thousands of miles in the winter and summer to follow the warm weather. We call this **migration**. They can feel the magnetic field of Earth and they use it to find their way.

These birds find their way by feeling the magnetic field of Earth.

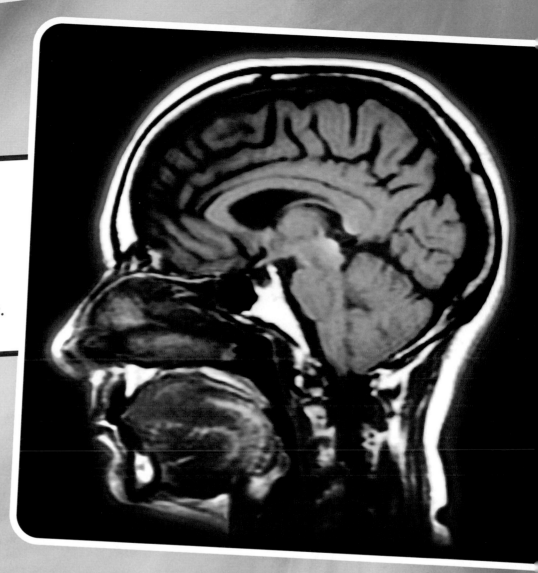

This picture of someone's head was taken using magnetism from an MRI machine.

Doctors can use a machine with a large magnet inside to take a picture of the inside of your body. This helps them to look for some illnesses or injuries.

The machine they use is called a magnetic resonance imaging machine, or MRI for short. The magnetism travels through your body and makes pictures to show what is inside.

Electromagnets

When electricity flows through a wire it makes a **magnetic field** just like the field from a magnet. This is called an **electromagnet**.

An electromagnet is useful because it can be switched on and off! You could make a simple electromagnet using a battery, some wire, and a nail.

If you wrap wire around an iron nail and connect the wire to a small battery you can make a simple electromagnet.

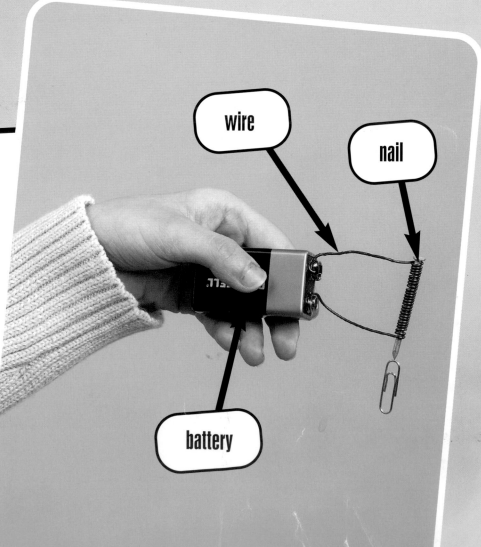

wire

nail

battery

Electromagnets can be used in scrapyards to pick up scrap **iron** and old cars. When the magnet is switched on it picks the scrap up so it can be moved to the place it needs to go. When the magnet is switched off, the **attractive force** also switches off and the scrap falls away.

A large electromagnet can be used to move scrap metal around a scrapyard.

Electromagnets can also be used as a lock to keep doors closed. The magnets on each side of the door pull towards each other so the door cannot be opened. When you swipe a card or use a special key, the magnet switches off and the door will open.

Magnets in motors

An electric **motor** is made with a coil of wire and a magnet. When **electricity** flows through the wire it makes a **magnetic field**. The magnetic field from the wire is pushed and pulled by the magnetic field from the magnets. This makes the coil of wire turn. The motor turns electricity into movement.

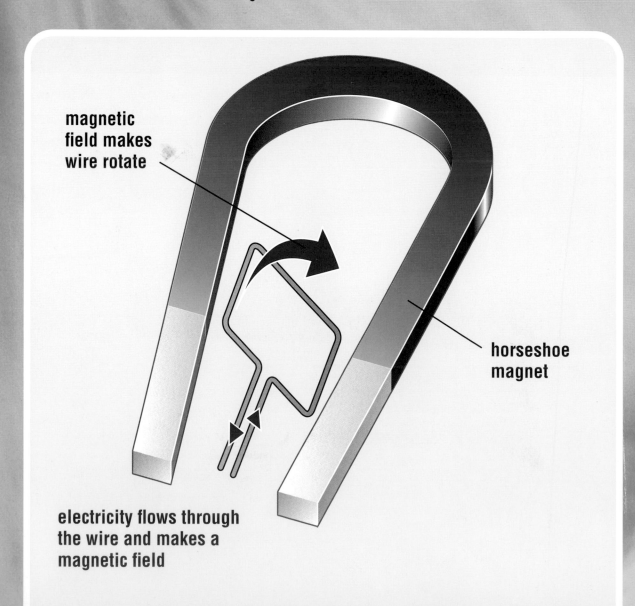

magnetic field makes wire rotate

horseshoe magnet

electricity flows through the wire and makes a magnetic field

Where would we be without motors?

Without electric motors there would be no DVD players, food mixers, washing machines, dishwashers, electric trains, CD players, or hairdryers.

This fan uses a motor to turn electricity into a spinning movement. When the motor turns it makes the blades of the fan turn. The blades push air forwards to cool you down.

Making electricity

Magnets can also be used to make **electricity**. If you move a magnet around some wire you make a small amount of electricity flow through the wire.

Some bicycles have a machine called a **dynamo** fixed to the wheels. As the bicycle wheels turn they make a magnet turn inside some coils of wire in the dynamo. This makes enough electricity to work the bicycle lights!

This is a wind-up radio. You wind it up by hand. As it unwinds, a magnet turns inside a coil of wire. This makes enough electricity to work the radio.

Most of the electricity we use every day is made using magnets. Power stations burn oil to heat up water, which makes clouds of steam. This steam has enough **energy** to turn large coils of wire around huge magnets. This makes the electricity that is carried along wires to our homes.

We use electricity for many things such as heating, lighting, and cooking. Electricity powers our computers and televisions. Where would we be without electricity?

Magnets and sound

We use speakers to listen to sound when we play a CD or watch television. A coil of wire inside the speaker carries electric **signals**. When **electricity** flows through the wire it gets pushed by the magnet around it.

The magnet pushes and pulls the wire in the same pattern as the electric signal coming into it. These pushes and pulls make the speaker **vibrate** and this makes the sound that we hear.

coil of wire

–

+

electric signals

speaker cone vibrates to make sound

When you use speakers to listen to music or the television you are using magnets to turn electric signals into sound.

Magnets are also used to record sound. Inside a microphone there is a moving coil of wire and a magnet. When you make a noise into the microphone the vibration of your voice makes the coil move. The coil moves inside the magnet and this makes electric signals that travel down the wires to be recorded.

A microphone turns sound into electric signals. A speaker turns electric signals back into sounds.

Magnetic information

Magnetic **material** can store information as a pattern. If you look at the back of a credit card you will find a black strip. Although the card is made of plastic, this part of the card is actually a magnetic code.

When you pay for something in a shop the card passes through a special machine. The machine can read the magnetic code so that it can tell who is paying.

The black strip on this card is a magnetic code.

If you record a television programme on to a videotape you are storing sounds and pictures as magnetic patterns. Computers also have a magnetic disk inside that stores lots of information.

This is the magnetic disk inside a computer. This is where information is stored and kept safe.

Imagine life without magnets

Magnets help us to save information and then play it back. Without magnets you would not be able to record your favourite TV programme or keep things safe on your computer.

Facts about magnets

In the United Kingdom, some coins are magnetic. Can you find out which ones?

In the United States none of the coins is magnetic, but magnetic ink is used to print bank notes!

One woman in the United States has collected over 35,000 fridge magnets. She must have a very large fridge!

The strength of a magnet is measured in Tesla (T) or Gauss (G).

Grapes are slightly repelled by very strong magnets called rare-earth magnets!

There is a magnetic fluid called ferrofluid that has tiny magnetic particles mixed in with it.

The word "magnet" comes from Magnesia in Greece where they were first discovered.

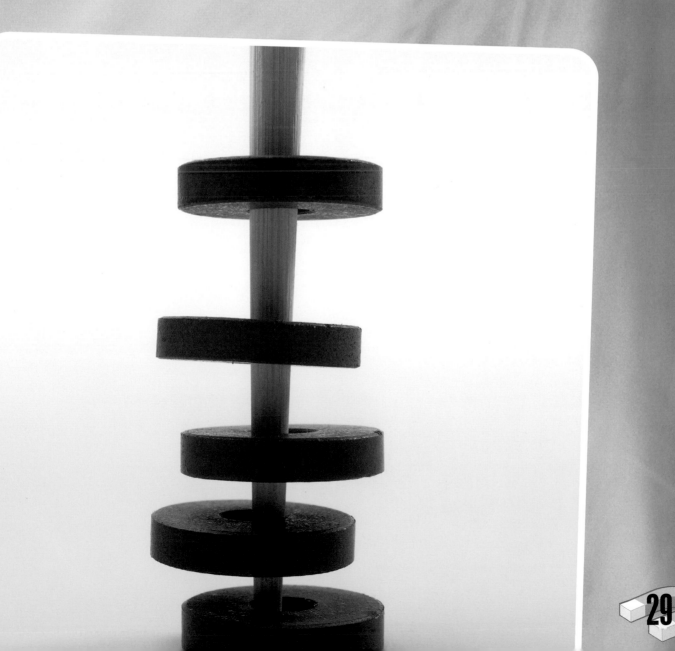

Find out more

You can find out more about science in everyday life by talking to your teacher or parents. Your local library will also have books that can help. You will find the answers to many of your questions in this book. If you want to know more, you can use other books and the Internet.

Books to read

Discovering Science: Electricity and Magnetism,
    Rebecca Hunter (Raintree, 2003)
Science Answers: Magnetism, Chris Cooper
    (Heinemann Library, 2003)
Science Files: Electricity and Magnetism,
    Steve Parker (Heinemann Library, 2004)

Using the Internet

Explore the Internet to find out more about magnets. Try using a search engine such as www.yahooligans.com or www.internet4kids.com, and type in keywords such as "**dynamo**", "**magnetic field**", and "**motor**".

Glossary

aluminium light metal that magnets will not stick to, some drink cans are made of aluminium

attractive force magnetic force that pulls two things together

compass machine with a small magnet inside that always points to north. You can use a compass to help find your way.

dynamo machine that you might find on a bike. When the wheels turn the movement makes electricity, usually for light.

electricity form of energy that can be used to make things work. Computers and televisions work using electricity.

electromagnet when electricity is used to make a magnet that can be switched on and off

energy power to make things work. You need energy to get up and walk or run around.

force push or pull

iron type of metal that is magnetic and can also be made into a magnet

magnetic domains small magnetic areas inside materials

magnetic field area around a magnet where the force of the magnet pushes and pulls

magnetism when something turns into a magnet

magnetize when a metal becomes a magnet

material something that objects are made from

melted when a solid is heated up and turns into a liquid

migration movement from one area to another. Some birds migrate in the winter to find warmer places to live.

motor machine that makes things move

recycle use the material from old things to make something new

repulsive force magnetic force that pushes two things apart

signal sign or message

steel type of metal that magnets will stick to, some drink cans are made of steel

surface top or outside part of an object

vibrate move up and down or backwards and forwards very quickly

Index

Titles in the *Science In Your Life* series include:

Hardback   1 184 443658 6

Hardback   1 844 43662 4

Hardback   1 844 43659 4

Hardback   1 844 43663 2

Hardback   1 844 43660 8

Hardback   1 844 43664 0

Hardback   1 844 43661 6

Find out about the other titles in this series on our website www.raintreepublishers.co.uk